INDIA AND CONSPIRACY

COMBINED EDITION

SARTHAK CHARAYA

Made with ♥ on the Notion Press Platform
www.notionpress.com

I dedicate this book to the two people I admire the most in my life-my mon and my dad. I thank my mom and my dad for their indomitable strength that protected the child I was. That protection allowed me to shape the individual in me and also for their strong determination and values in life, which influence that individual to become better.

Contents

1

Satanic Musicians

It might be possible that Honey Singh is 'SATANIC'. All of you who don't know 'What is SATAN or SATANISM?', I'll tell you in the easiest way. The prince of evil spirit is SATAN, you can take it as the opposite of GOD. In this world, the biggest evil being is SATAN. I'll give you a little bit of basic knowledge about SATANISM by which it will be much easier to know this theory. In satanic language hand signs are used.

And whom you have seen using these signs most commonly? **"Honey Singh"**. Many religions and religious books have mentioned SATAN. But

Talking about India, it consists mainly of Hindus and in Hindu culture, there's nothing about Satan. Here, nobody knows about Satan or Satanism. You can assume it is like when the song 'SATAN' by Honey Singh came, many people were pronouncing it **(satn - सतन)**. But the main point is why the song was named 'SATAN'. In the song, it doesn't consist of anything related to satan. It is said that satan has less power because of its less follower and the people who follow SATAN, try their best to make other people join their group and to find people who can start following Satanism.

Just imagine when this song was released, people started getting to know about honey's new song named 'SATAN'. And people were going on google and started searching SATAN, but they were getting the song spite of that they were getting to know about the real

SATAN. By this many people must have explored SATANISM. We can say that honey Singh is promoting SATAN. SATAN spreads evil ideology. It teaches evil things and makes people self-destructive. It forces its followers to the wrong path. The same is done by Honey Singh, things like parties, drugs, girls, liquor, etc. All these messages are spread by Honey Singh through his songs. I have seen him rarely spreading any good message, earlier, he used to have a good vibe in his songs. He also had created a song on 'BHAGAT SINGH', But that album or that song didn't work. It is said that most musicians and famous personalities have traded their souls with SATAN in exchange for fame and success. This is true, it is admitted by many musicians. It is done, like the person who wants to be famous or needs success on a high level, he can trade his soul with SATAN. According to theory, earlier when Honey Singh was not going well. It can be possible that he might have sold his soul to SATAN in exchange for fame and success.

This is just a theory.

SATAN has 1 number that is '**666**'. Recently, Honey Singh was not well. And now he has come back and he has told that he used to get scared of small things like his own shadow, his family members, etc. We can say that he might have lost control over himself. And it used to happen when you have done a deal with SATAN and later on, you have started running out of it.

I can't even imagine what he had gone through at that point of time. When he came out in public, he was very specific that he was disappeared for 18 months. And the period of 18 months was mentioned again and again. Like, As I have told you that SATAN's number is '666'. And when you add 6,6 and 6. You get 18. I know that this is a crazy theory, but I tell you that sit with a peaceful mind and again think about it.

2

India's Area 51

———◆♡◆———

India can have its own **AREA 51**. For those who don't know what is AREA 51, it was an area that was kept concealed for a long period by **U.S** Govt. Slowly people started discovering that area and later on govt. also admitted this place. It is said that weapon testing is done there, new-age weapons are also created, and even talking with aliens is done there. But in reality, what is going on at that place, nobody knows. But lately, a new conspiracy theory has come out that India has the same place as this in **KONGKA LA**(at the border of China). People who live near that place have told that they have seen UFOs coming out of the land and going inside it. People have seen UFOs through google maps. And they have also seen military camps.

It is said, that area is run by both countries(**INDIA** and **CHINA**). When people ask the person who is guarding that area " are they real UFOs?" they reply by saying "No, they are just Chinese fire lanterns"

But are they really Chinese fire lanterns or UFOs?

3

Alien Invasion In India

———◦♭◦———

Now, if we are talking about aliens so, it might be possible that INDIA had been visited by aliens.

On December 18,2012

11:25 AM,

In **Jodhpur,**

There was one sonic boom. A sonic boom is a phenomenon in which there is a huge impact due to high speed which breaks the sound barrier. And do it a huge-huge noise is created. And it is fucking loud!!

It is usually in jet planes when they used to travel at high speed.

So, when this sonic boom happened in Jodhpur. Many people assume that the air force is doing a testing of a new aircraft. And it can be possible that the sonic boom must have come from the aircraft. Later, when it was asked by the air force then they replied "no, there is nothing like that. And even if we test anything we keep a radius of 60km from public areas."

Airforces clearly denied that this phenomenon was not done by the air forces. So, who the fuck did this?

And then, many theories came up that it can be possible that It can be a UFO'S. Because sonic booms are created at a very high speed and our jets are not that fast that gets instantly vanish after that. As the sonic boom happened people came out to see and many were already out and they saw nothing. It has to be a UFO.

But just imagine you are inside your home and you listen to a sonic boom. And when you go out, you see nothing.

4

Nine Unknown Mens

———◦♭◦———

When it comes to history throughout the ages, it's safe to say that we know way less than we don't. While it can be attributed to a lack of information, for the most part, some areas were designed such, that prohibited commoners from getting to know about them.

Secret societies have been a part and parcel of advanced civilizations throughout the ages, and the ever-present veil of mystery shrouding them can be attributed to their descriptor itself - they are, after all, supposed to be '**secret**'. Be it the **Illuminati**, or the Priory Of Sion, multiple secret societies existed, and apparently, they are the ones who have actually been running the world, away from the commoners' gaze.

When it comes to India, we apparently have one of the oldest and most important secret societies, called '**The 9 Unknown Men**', which was set up by **Ashoka the Great**, more than 2000 years ago. It is said that Emperor Ashoka believed that knowledge is power, and the key to preserving that power is to collect, nurture, and use knowledge in a way that can be used for great deeds, but can also prove to be terrible if exposed to the wrong hands. So, he summoned nine of the most brilliant minds in India at the time, from various fields and disciplines, to form a secret society called '**The Nine Unknown Men**'.

However, it was designed in such a way that should a member quit because of death, disease, or other reasons, a worthy member would be chosen in his place as the successor, and the society would continue with the pattern of having exactly nine members at any given point in time.

There were nine disciplines based on the expertise of which, the nine were chosen. They were **Propaganda, Physiology, Microbiology, Alchemy, Communication, Gravity, Cosmogony, Light, and Sociology.**

Between these 9 disciplines, everything that a strong ruler needed to be all-powerful, was covered. There were subjects in between these nine disciplines that were controversial, mysterious, and sometimes also referred to as '**forbidden**'.

For example, how to kill someone with only one touch, also called '**The Touch Of Death**' was studied. It is said that modern-day Judo originated from the leaked knowledge of this very stream. Other topics include communication in its most advanced form, which apparently also dealt with extraterrestrial communication with aliens. Alchemy includes the transmutation of metals, the most popular form of which is converting metals to gold.

The most interesting thing? They say the most famous and influential people in history, mostly scientists and artists, have invariably been part of secret societies. Apparently, **Isaac Newton, Albert Einstein**, as well as our very own **APJ Abdul Kalam** were members of Ashoka's Nine Unknown Men.

Was mind blown?

5

JANA GANA MANA

——◦▷◦——

The controversy over the National Anthem of India is an old one. And I can see a pattern in happenings that highlights the confusion about Tagore's patriotism.

The Bengali song "**Jana Gana Mana**" was written in 1911, but it was largely unknown to the readers of the Brahmo Samaj journal, **Tattwabodhini Patrika**, of which Tagore was the editor.

Jana Gana Mana was sung on 27 December 1911 at the **Indian National Congress, Calcutta**, and again in January 1912 at the annual event of the **Adi Brahmo Samaj**.

Although this controversy shadowed Jana Gana Mana on 27 December 1911 itself as Emperor George V was scheduled to arrive in the city on 30 December and a section of the Anglo-Indian English press in Calcutta thought – and duly reported – that Tagore's hymn was a homage to the emperor.

A letter from 1939:

"I should only insult myself if I cared to answer those who consider me capable of such unbounded stupidity."

Another letter from Tagore to **Pulin Behari Sen**:

"A certain high official in His Majesty's service, who was also my friend, had requested that I write a song of felicitation towards the Emperor. The request simply amazed me. It caused a great stir in my heart. In response to that great mental turmoil, I pronounced the victory in Jana Gana Mana of that Bhagya Vidhata (ed. God of Destiny) of

India who has from age after age held steadfast the reins of India's chariot through rise and fall, through the straight path and the curved. That Lord of Destiny, that Reader of the Collective Mind of India, that Perennial Guide, could never be George V, George VI, or any other George. Even my official friend understood this about the song. After all, even if his admiration for the crown was excessive, he was not lacking in simple common sense."

Tagore said his official friend didn't lack common sense, which suggests that others who believe in this controversy lack common sense.

While in reality, common sense is subjective and depends on how well the person in question knows the topic in question.

It is quite obvious that people haven't read much about Tagore and mostly don't even know who wrote our National Anthem (even many don't know the difference between National Anthem and National Song).

And anyone unaware of the spirit of the writer can easily misinterpret the song. A common example is that people have an emotional attachment to songs as they have linked the lyrics with someone or something in their life experience. And that incident not necessarily corresponds with the incident writer had in mind from his experience while writing the song.

Similarly, the controversial part "**Bharat Bhagya Vidhata**" of Jana Gana Mana can have many interpretations depending on the listener.

Bharat Bhagya Vidhata simply means the God (writer/maker/creator) of the Destiny of India.

Anyone having faith in British Monarchy would have obviously interpreted it as George V, while another person can interpret it as freedom fighters, someone having faith in God will interpret it as God, while anyone else being optimistic about the future can interpret it as adults or children population of the country, some can even interpret it as any political figure.

So, this controversy is neither false nor true. It is just a variation in understanding of the song. Which is one of the disadvantages of using interpretable language.

6

Subliminal Messages in Indian Ads

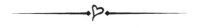

There is nobody who uses advertising these days who is not using subliminal tactics to get their message across these days. That doesn't mean they are using masked or ultrasonic subliminal messaging, but advertisers do take full advantage of the ease with which one can create a subliminal impact on your thinking and choices. It's long since been used in mainstream advertising for decades now.

Just the simple act of repeatedly watching a commercial enough times has such an effect. The increased volume of commercials communicates things to the subconscious ("This is urgent, pay attention!"). The things they show in the background. The selective use of blur and focus. The music they use influences your memory, associations and emotions. The people they show, what their body language is, what they're doing, the expressions on their faces, how they're interacting with a responding to the product, and on and on - all of this has subliminal impact on the viewer. That's why they use it.

They don't need to use subliminal audio in advertising to get much the same effect. Why bother, especially when subliminal audio in advertising is not legal?

So how does the government use this? Advertising to join the military. Advertising for political candidates. And the news media outlets are a big one. The news media is usually owned by special interests who work with the government to shape what you see and hear in the news, and what you believe. That's why we have so few news media outlets in the United States that give you real news instead of telling you to favor the point of view of the political "Left" or the "Right".

Believe me... they don't need subliminal audio like what you're talking about to get the same results. And the best thing is, you don't even know it's happening; they can do all this influencing and the typical person seeks it out and eats it up!

That's why it wasn't long after starting to work in the field of making subliminal messaging for a living that I stopped watching TV and especially the "news". I don't listen to the radio, and I don't read magazines. This sort of influence is everywhere these days, and even without doing any of those things, I am still bombarded with it in stores, on billboards, signs, before movies and online.

The government has been doing this for decades, and so have companies and advertisers.

There many examples related to this like, **Ranbir Kapoor Coca-Cola** ad, **Siddharth Malhotra wild stone** ad, etc.

These all passes sexual message. Just observe the expressions and body language of the actor's. You will also get to know about it.

7

Is INDIA still a British Dominion?

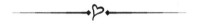

All laws by British Crown still are applicable like Indian Police Act (1857) , Indian Penal Code etc,

India became "Republic Within Commonwealth on 1950", now what is republic? Republic simply means rule of law but note WITHIN ,one cannot be free if they are within other's jurisdiction not matter how many constitutions you write.

On 2nd September 1953,Dr.Ambedkar clarified in the Rajya Sabha (Parliament) that "People always keep on saying to me, so you are the maker of the Constitution. My answer is I was a hack. What I was asked to, I did much against my will. I am quite prepared to say that I shall be the first person to burn it. It does not suit anybody."

India is a Commonwealth Nation making its citizens "Commonwealth Citizens" and establishes Queen as our Head. When Queen came to India her name was written on top of Indian President and she can travel to any commonwealth nation without passport and visa because these nations are her common wealth.

In 1947 Nehru signed "Transfer of Power Agreement" with Britishers and this agreement hasn't been disclosed to people of India even after 60 years. Everytime a Prime Minister is Sworn in ,he sings on this agreement that is never ever shown to anybody except PM and President.

India is among the British Accredited Registry BAR Council jurisdiction. Indian Courts cite British Laws if corresponding law is not found regarding a case. This makes it clear that Present British Laws apply on all Indians.

India word itself is a creation of Britishers and as long we register our names in Birth Certificate to this entity we will always be slave of British Crown.

8
The Burari Death

The Burari deaths case was a terrifying incident back in 2018 where 11 members of a family in Burari, Delhi had killed themselves. Many call it to be a case of mass suicide. While very little is known about the case, most of the information stands baseless or unreasonable, as television media often portrays. A family with a deep inside story was revealed to the world much better because of Leena Yadav's documentary on Netflix titled, 'House of Secrets: the Burari Deaths'. Until a death in 2007, the Chundawats (familiarly called the Bhatia family), were like any other middle-class family, settled and focused on a better future. While many who viewed the family from the outside thought they had found consolation in spirituality, there is no one left to describe what happened behind the four walls of the Burari house. The present article highlights the much-discussed case from different angles and information that were available, to make the reader understand the story behind the closed doors of the 11-member family.

On 1ˢᵗ July 2018, when the neighbours, Gurcharan Singh, Kuldeep Singh, and Pritpal Kaur went to check on the Bhatia family (originally Chundawat), who owned a grocery shop and had neither opened the same in the morning (which generally used to open at 5:30 AM) nor had collected milk from the daily milk-man and were not responding to the neighbours' calls, they found the main door open as it was not locked from inside. As they went upstairs, they were left shocked to discover nine family members hanging from an iron grill on the ceiling of the roof in a circular formation. The tenth member, a lady, was hanging right opposite them and their mother was lying in the other room, on the floor, near her bed. The family members were blindfolded, hands and feet bound, while they had hanged themselves. The family's dog, the only member alive, was tied to the roof and was said to be barking continuously.

Three generations lived together in the same house. All of the members were well-educated and well-adjusted social members. It was a family of 11 members who was living in that house in Burari, Delhi. The matriarch, Narayani Devi, was a widow who was a mother of three sons and two daughters, among which two sons and one daughter used to reside with her in that house. Bhuvnesh was the elder son and Lalit was the youngest. Both were married to Savita and Tina respectively. While Bhuvnesh and Savita had two daughters and one son (Maneka, Neetu, and Dhruv), Lalit and Tina were parenting one son only, Shivam. Narayani Devi's daughter Pratibha was the mother of her only daughter Priyanka.

The family had a general store and the younger son, Lalit had a plywood business. Neighbours have claimed that the family was doing fairly well in both their businesses. Professed to be religious people, neighbours, relatives and associated colleagues claimed that the 11-member family involved nice, generous, and harmonious people who were never involved in fights amongst each other or with people around. While the children in the family were intelligent, good in academics, and offered respectful behaviour, the other members were eager to help their relatives and friends whenever in need. Sujata Nagpal, the surviving sister, and eldest brother, Dinesh, agreed to the opinions of the neighbours about her family when she was asked about the same. None of the family relatives were accepting the fact that the 11-member daily had attempted a mass suicide. This was major because the family had thrown a huge celebration for one of their daughters, Priyanka's engagement, which happened exactly 14 days before the occurrence of the discussed incident.

Rajeev Tomar, Head Constable, Burari Police Station (2017-2020) and also the family's former neighbour was the first one to be informed about the horrific incident which was presumed to be a suicide initially. Tomar witnessed the aforementioned happenings and believed that the mass suicide formation depicted a banyan tree. When Manoj Kumar, Station House Officer (SHO), Burari Police Station (2016-2019) approached the crime scene with his team, he claimed to have never witnessed such an incident in his entire career. Witnessing a lack of circumstantial evidence contributing to the alleged mass killing, no sign of burglary as the women were wearing all their ornaments and absence of signs calling the incident to be a suicide as the members were blindfolded along with a lack of suicide note, the police officers were perplexed with more questions than answers. Since the family-owned grocery store is often crowded in the morning time, the news of the incident started spreading like forest fires which was an add-on challenge for the investigators. Media reporters and curiosity among residents nearby and around the locality had all gathered to take a glimpse of the unusual occurrence. Therefore, controlling the crowd and safeguarding the crime scene was of foremost importance and the same was dutifully carried out by the Delhi Police.

Forensic Science Laboratory, Delhi (FSL) was informed of the spine-chilling incident after which they arrived with their expert team. Both FSL and the police investigators believed that the motive behind the happening of the incident was to be known. The police officials during the investigation period took into account the footage of a CCTV camera which was positioned in one of the walls of the house, front-facing the lane, which was checked from the previous night till the time of the incident. This was carried out to rule out the possibility of an outsider's entry and to ensure that no outsider had their involved in the incident that took place.

Because of the surviving family members' claim, a murder case was registered by the police initially, although the latter had dissented with the former. In the FIR lodged by the police officials, the entire incident and the evidence taken care of were detailed.

The bodies of the 11 members were properly packed before they were sent to the mortuary. They were brought down by the police officials only. The post-mortem reports revealed that the deaths of the members were due to hanging only. The eldest member of the family, Narayani Devi had died due to partial hearing. The presence of faecal matter (digested, solid waste) in the large intestine of all the dead members suggested that no one was stressed. The case was further shifted to Dr, Deputy Commissioner of Police, Crime Branch, Delhi, and his team.

When the crime branch took into account every minute detailing in the house where the incident had taken place, they believed concerning a few things which were:

1. The elder son, Bhuvnesh had tried to set his hands, which were tried, free, as clear signs of struggle could be seen in his fingers.
2. The children of the house were tied not only by their hands but also by their feet, ruthlessly with telephone wires. There were no signs of struggle by any of them. Both eyes and mouths were tapped and their ears were stuffed with cotton.
3. The eldest member of the family, Narayani Devi was found lying dead in the other room beside her bed with a half-turned body. There was a belt around her neck which resulted in a few marks on the side of her neck.
4. Everyone in the family had a scarf around their neck, which was used to hang themselves.
5. Evidence of a ritual that was performed the night before was discovered as well. A leftover ritual pyre was found. From the ashes that were lying around the pyre, it was clear that the same was used a day before the incident.
6. On 28th June 2018 (as the CCTV camera had shown), Tina, Lalit's wife, and her son, Shivam were seen to have purchased four stools. Further, on 30th June 2018 at 9:40 PM, Tina was seen to be carrying some newly purchased tools with Neetu. At 10:29 PM, Lalit's son, Shivam, was seen opening their plywood shop and carrying a small bundle of wires upstairs.

7. A packet of milk was kept in the fridge for the following day's usage, and Lalit, the family's youngest son, had recharged the phones of other family members the day before the event. In the kitchen, soaked chana dal (black gramme) was discovered, most likely for the next day's supper.
8. A register was found beside the temple in the house. After a rigorous search, 11 diaries were discovered where the earliest entry was dated 2007 and the last entry was made the night before the incident (2018).

The Story behind 11 diaries

1. The crime branch had opined that the language that was used in the diaries was instructional, commanding, and conversational. The last page of the diary had all the instructions that needed to be followed by the family, and that eventually unfolded to become a horrifying incident.
2. The first mention of Bhopal Singh in Lalit's diaries occurs on September 7, 2007, when the notes asked the family to remember him by keeping his black-and-white photograph in front of them. The September message stated, *"Mann Mein Dhyan yahi rakho ki Daddy meri purani aadatein chhut jaye"* [pray that you get rid of your old habits].
3. On 24th June 2018, the last diary entry that was made explained a ritual called "Banyan Tree Ritual" which would run for a period of seven days along with the puja called, Badh Puja. Badh is originally a tree that has its roots hanging from the branches. The time of the incident was mentioned in the diary (supposedly at 1 AM).
4. Concerning the Badh Puja, it was instructed that;

i. The same would be religiously carried out for a period of seven days and if anybody would have come to visit the family then the puja was supposed to take place the following day.

ii. It was directed that nothing related to the puja should be visible to any of the outsiders coming to the house.

iii. Dim light should be used in the puja and eyes should be completely shut.

iv. The blindfold should be properly tied in the eyes, the mouth should be gagged by a handkerchief, and the mind should be focused and empty. The eldest member, Narayani Devi was directed to complete the ritual by lying down only as she was aged and overweight.

v. It was directed that while performing the puja, it should be imagined that the branches of the tree were wrapping themselves around an individual's body. The ritual should therefore be performed with unity and determination, which will help repent mistakes.

1. The diaries mentioned every little and minute detail that the family was abiding by in order to conduct their lives. The diaries also had indications of the family conducting witchcraft and occult practices. It felt as if some third person or mystical energy was directing the 11 members thereby controlling them.

6. Although the crime branch had tried to contact some person with a religious or a spiritual background who were related to the family, their efforts went down the drain as no such contact was available.

The Bhatia family was headed by Bhopal Singh, the husband of Narayani Devi who had died in 2007. After his dismissal, the family was leftover with no one who could control it or be an authoritative figure to control the ups and downs associated with it. Clinical hypnotherapist Anita Anand claimed that in a typical Indian family when the patriarch dies, there is a vacuum in the family. A somewhat similar kind of incident could be noticed in this case. Bhopal Singh, until his death, used to control the family, their planning, children's education, etc. The responsibilities that Bhopal

Singh used to swiftly carry out landed on his youngest son, Lalit's shoulders, after his death. Friends and relatives of Lalit voiced that it was because of his maturity and decision-making skills which made other family members follow him and treat his sayings as supreme ones. It is to be noted that neighbours, friends, and relatives of the family have repeatedly agreed to the fact that the deceased Bhopal Singh was a very nice, broad-minded human being and therefore it was unlikely of he expressed such commands.

Entry in the diary started right after Bhopal Singh's death and the majority of the directions and diary entries were concerning Lalit. As the investigation proceeded, experts and state actors came to recognize the youngest son of Narayani Devi, Lalit to be the mind behind the Burari incident. Lalit was supposedly involved in direct communication with his deceased father in his dreams where his father used to tell him how to conduct the family and the same was followed. He started sharing these conversations with his family. It was Neetu, one of the children who had informed the neighbours that her uncle, Lalit, was possessed by their grandfather's spirit and it was the latter that guided them. Whenever Lalit used to converse with his family about the instructions he received from his dead father, his voice used to change to that of his father's. The diary mentioned that the deceased father's spirit would visit the family every Tuesday, Thursday, Saturday, and Sunday. The instructions that were given resulted in the financial well-being of the family. This made the family believe whatever the deceased father was directing. It was promised that the deceased father, Bhopal Singh was supposed to visit the family after a complete section of the Banyan Tree ritual and save the family members. The irony was although the family was made to believe that they will be saved, they eventually called their death all by themselves.

Savita and Tina, Narayani Devi's daughters-in-law, fulfilled the stereotype of capable housewives. They got up early, prepared food for the family, looked after the youngsters and the elderly and were kind and well-behaved to everyone they encountered.

Dr Virendra Singh, Handwriting Division, Forensics Science Lab, Delhi was provided with the copies and diaries that were discovered in the Bhatia family's house for identifying the handwriting in the entries. It was revealed that Pratibha's daughter, Priyanka, and Bhuvnesh's daughter, Neetu, were the ones who were writing these notes.

As it slowly came out to the experts involved in the present case that Lalit was the one behind the incident, they could gradually read the minds of Lalit and the thought process he had been going through. In many ways, he had felt out of control, as has been explained by clinical hypnotherapist Anita Anand.

The Chundawats changed their way of life as well. They ceased to consume and prepare non-vegetarian meals. At home, Bhavnesh quit drinking. Pujas became a common occurrence. The number of stores expanded from one to three, including Lalit's plywood shop, Bhavnesh's grocery store, and the third one they were opening jointly, as well as the house's floors.

After the ground investigation was completed, the crime branch decided to go for a psychological autopsy in which a group of scientists and psychologists go into the minds of the dead individuals to find out what had happened. It was Lalit who had psychosis and he was slowly transmitting it to his family members, making it a case of shared psychosis. This was why the family members had started believing Lalit blindly. It was discovered that the family had not planned to commit suicide, instead, it was the circumstances that made them do so. The crime branch had concluded the three-year-old investigation stating that the Burari death case was neither a murder nor a suicide as there was no foul play involved, it was specifically an accidental death that had taken place. The eldest brother had donated the eyes of the family members before cremating them.

Rumours and Stories which feed common people's mind

1. Reporters had noticed 11 pipes (7 facing downwards and 4 facing straight) in one of the bare walls of the house where the family

used to reside and the place of occurrence of the incident. They had related the same with the fact that the 11 members of the Bhatia family who had died, consisted of seven females and four males. As a matter of fact, was that the pipes were placed in a similar way in which the family had tied themselves to the iron ceiling. The news which was shown in the television media claimed that the pipes were fitted to let the 11 souls escape, although the person who had installed the pipes aired away such claims and firmly believed that the pipes were installed for light and ventilation.

2. 11 grills were present in the main entrance door of the house and 11 rods in the railing of the terrace. Along with the same the house had exactly 11 windows and vents. The idea behind the same was that the number 11 had significance and deep relevance to the Burari incident.

The plumber who had fitted the pipes in the house, his daughter, Geeta Mata, was unnecessarily dragged into the incident and was related to being a Tantrik who was responsible for the death of the 11 members. The media interviewed the woman and declared her to be associated with black magic, just because she was dressed in red clothes. Geeta Mata was referred to as the family's spiritual guru although she burst all bubbles relating to the Burari incident and claimed that she was unnecessarily harassed by the media.

9
The Monkey Man

———◦♡◦———

The recent monster-inspired panic in India has historical precedents, such as Spring-Heeled Jack, but has been more dangerous than most of them.

Descriptions of the Monkey Man of India, first mentioned in police calls on May 13, 2001, have shown little consistency. So far, some described the entity as having a metal claw or claws, while others likened it to a cat with glowing eyes. Another claimed it had flaming red eyes and that green lights glowed upon its chest. These descriptions were but a few among many.

Whether the creature that so many feared was like a monkey is a matter of dispute. Witness claims also described it as agile and feline, as a bandaged figure, or as a helmeted thing.

Even more unusual theories made it out to be a foreign robot assassin. A thirty-five-year-old shopkeeper named Anim Keshri thought it to be a remote-controlled computerized creature -- since how else could it leap four stories and disappear?

May Mayhem

During May, dozens of individuals were said to have been hurt in its attacks, and two took fatal leaps because they heard the "monster" was nearby. In daily newspapers, photos of scratched victims upset New Delhi residents.

Early during the flap, on the night of May 14, fifty attacks were reported, according to the May 17 edition of *The Australian.* (Numbers vary widely in news reports.) The scare had at this point moved from its origins in Ghaziabad to a number of areas in East Delhi.

Early May 15, at 2:30 A.M., a pregnant woman in East Delhi fell down some stairs after being awakened by the shouts of neighbors saying that the monkey had arrived. She died in a hospital, having been one of the two aformentioned jumping fatalities. That same night (late Monday/early Tuesday), police received 13 distress calls from the New Usmanpur area.

As of May 17, police in Delhi had taken more than 40 -- perhaps as many as 65 according to other accounts -- calls reporting depredations of this alleged Monkey Man since May 13, from many sections of the city.

Third World Tensions

Contributing to the situation were three factors that afflict Third World cities in particular: the presence of many illiterate and superstitious rural immigrants, a modern mass media, and a high population density. These added to the elements that could inflame imaginations in the hot darkness.

"Jokes" increased the tension. In Nangloi, a rat bite was claimed to be the work of the Monkey Man. (That surely must have left everyone laughing.)

One doctor was arrested on May 19 after having scared his neighbors by throwing down an inflated surgical glove which had been smeared with brown hair dye.

A senior police officer of the Delhi police, quoted in the *Daily Pioneer* circa May 16, said, "The whole drama was very carefully enacted by the anti-social elements who wanted to test the nerves of the Delhi Police." They blamed this alleged sabotage on Pakistan's Inter Services Intelligence, for whom the "mischief mongers" were reportedly causing the terror.

A nine-year-old named Arjun Bajaj believes the Monkey Man is a black-masked fellow with springs in his shoes -- and a button which he uses to vanish. Bajaj admits to thinking that perhaps the first one was the doctor with the glove, but is frightened of others like him.

Elements of Legend

It seems probable that elements of the mace-equipped Hindu monkey god of legend, Hanuman, have found their way into the public's conceptions because of his monkey elements -- with his mace being related to the metal claw of the alleged Monkey Man. Other contributing factors include sleeping outdoors, heat, darkness, crowding and fearfulness, which combine to increase the panic. Suresh Roy, police Joint Commissioner in Delhi, spoke to ABCNEWS.com about how seriously the resultant injuries had to be taken. Police have been posted on rooftops, areas have been kept well lit from dusk to dawn despite the routine power cuts, and border checks have been instituted at the city's points of entry. Public meetings have also been organized. What is more, Delhi police have been told to shoot the Monkey Man on sight.

Roy told the Reuters news agency that bites attributed to the thing were actually animal bites, according to consulted physicians.

Two "identikit" portraits that have been made of the "entity" are not really monkey-like, as one shows a staring hairy "man" with a swarthy complexion and flat nose, while the other one shows a narrow-faced, mustached "man" in dark glasses.

But if the being is a man, "he" is a short one, about four feet tall. "He" does not act like a monkey. Real monkeys have, of course, jumped on pedestrians and invaded homes, but have not attacked in the manner of the entity reported in Delhi.

Mass Confusion

In all this confusion, false identifications have been made. A four-foot-tall wandering Hindu mystic named Jamir was beaten up by residents of the nearby suburb of Noida, before being handed over to police.

A van driver in Delhi was set upon and given multiple fractures in the early A.M. hours of Friday, May 18, by people who thought him to be the Monkey Man.

Three thousand extra men in Delhi were assigned by police, as of May 21, to track down the Monkey Man. Police also offered a reward equaling $1,065 U.S. dollars (in rupees) for the creature's capture.

The terror has spread beyond that city, but with a difference.

Villagers in Assam have been terrorized by a wolflike Bear Man. As of May 27, more than a dozen people claimed they were attacked by it. The creature is alleged to make itself invisible before its attacks, and it is said to vanish when trapped in a ray of light. (There were power outages in Assam as well.) The Army, after investigation, could not substantiate any of these peoples' claims. The Assam Science Society, likewise, dismissed any such creature's existence in the district.

Kalyan Chakravarty, the Deputy Commissioner in Assam, noted the fueling of the panic by the Delhi Monkey Man stories. The *Indian Express* newspaper reported that villagers in the Nalbari district have, like their Delhi counterparts, organized watch groups.

Explanations abound. Nirmal Ghosh, in the May 23 *Straits Times,* writes about how the Monkey Man appeared to be a combination of much of what frightens people: its eyes were red and glowed, it could alter its shape, it was strong and agile, and it could see in the darkness -- it was thus a mixture of beast, criminal and supernatural being. Things were out of control for those who thought they saw it, because of their conditions of poverty, and this only increased their anxieties.

Whatever the explanation(s), the beast seems amazingly malleable and, indeed, prolific. One Delhi resident spoke how it was a monkey until it turned into a cat when grabbed. (It was, of course, likely a feline in the first place.) One criminal took advantage of the situation. He wore a mask so that witnesses would think that he was just one more Monkey Man.

What could well have started as some monkeys in Ghaziabad may have later been abetted, like in the above case, by humans. By

May 23, 324 police complaints had been received in Delhi, of which 260 were discovered to be hoaxes. By that time, officers considered the Monkey Man to be a man, not any other creature.

10
Nidhivan Temple

Nidhi Van is one of the most mysterious places located in the sacred city of Vrindavan, dedicated solely to Lord Krishna and his Gopis. There is a small temple in the middle of the area surrounded by a large forest which is said to have 'dancing trees' entangled with one another. Some say they are Krishan's Gopi's portraying the emotion of love for each other. The legend about Nidhi Van goes as; there was adivine saint "Swami Haridas" used to please his Lord Banke Bihari (Krishan Ji) by pouring the melodious rapture of his thrilling music in Nidhivan. And kind Bihari ji appear in his dream and also blessed him by appearing in the ground of Nidhivan and there is a temple at that place inside Nidhivan named **Prakatya Sathal** (place of appearance of shree Bihari ji).

'Madhuvan Main Jo Kanhaiya Kisi Gopi Se Mile
Kabhi Muskaaye Kabhee Chhede Kabhee Baat Kare
Radha Kaise Na Jale, Radha Kaise Na Jale
Aag Tan Man Me Lage
Radha Kaise Na Jale, Radha Kaise Na Jale'

Have you ever heard this song? This song says that Radha, Krishna and Gopinis meet everyday in Madhuvan. Do you think it is real?

Yes, it is true that Radha, Krishna and Gopinis appear every night in Madhuban. They dance together as they did in Dwapar Yuga.

It is extremely believed by the people of Vrindavan that Krishna and Radha every night appear and play Raas Lila in Madhuban.

Madhuban forest is popularly known as Nidhivan. It lies in Vrindavan city of Mathura district in Uttar Pradesh, India. This is the place where Lord Krishna played his pastimes in Dwapar Yuga. But do you believe he along with Radha and other Gopinis still appears there? This story has been featured by Aja Tak Channel of India also.

Nidhi van is surrounded by Bhusal {Tulsi} trees. In the middle of the forest there is a temple of Radha and Krishna. There is a one room Kunj also in a separate spot where Radha and Krishna take rest after dancing. The priest keeps brushes and waters every night before closing the temple. In the morning they seem to be used.

If you reach Nidhi van, you can see couple of trees connected everywhere. It is said that each tree represents Radha and Krishna. The forest is full of monkeys. People say that all trees become Gopinis at night. And the monkeys and any other animals and insects will disappear.

During the day, the spot is full of devotees. After 5 PM the temple will be closed and after 8 p.m., all creatures, human or animal, clear out of the vicinity after the night arti (prayer) as it is said that Lord Krishan and his Gopis perform their Ras-Lila (a dance form) there during sun-down and by morning all the goodies left back by the priest for t the celestial beings to feast on is vanished. Also, if anybody is left behind the next morning is found in such a state that he has no re-collection of what happened, i.e. they are found deaf, blind, dumb or dead. FACT.

Thus, we can also say that if these ancient myths are witnessed by millions even in today's date, then they aren't legends any more. They are hard core facts.

11
Khalistan Movement

———•ᗡ•———

Starting in the early 1980s, radical separatists spearheaded a bloody campaign to carve out an independent, theocratic Sikh state known as Khalistan (Land of the Pure) in Punjab and other parts of Northern India.

The roots of Khalistan lie in the British colonial policies of the late 1800s and early 1900s that sought to divide Sikhs and Hindus. **<u>Sikhs were recruited into the British army</u>** in large numbers to use against Hindu rulers that rebelled against the British Raj. Subsequently, after Indian independence in 1947, tensions between the state of Punjab and the central Indian government surfaced, leading to grievances amongst many Sikhs against the Indian government.

Punjab, for instance, was trifurcated into the states of Punjab, Haryana, and Himachal Pradesh in 1966, along linguistic lines (Punjab as a Punjabi speaking state, and Haryana and Himachal Pradesh as Hindi speaking states), which created resentment amongst many Sikhs that the historic contours of Punjab were being further divided after it has already been divided between India and Pakistan in 1947. Interestingly, it was the later division of Punjab that allowed Sikhs to enjoy a religious majority in the state, given the predominantly Hindu populations in Haryana and Himachal Pradesh.

Many Sikhs in Punjab also resented sharing the joint capital of Chandigarh with Haryana, and viewed water sharing agreements with Haryana as unfair and favoring farmers there to the detriment of those in Punjab. Sikh religious leaders were additionally apprehensive of the community **losing its identity and culture**, and wanted greater state powers for Punjab.

Although these types of issues often **mark normal state-federal government relations** in newly independent countries such as India, they were perceived by many Sikhs as religiously motivated policies of discrimination against them and were exploited by radical leaders, who built a narrative that Sikh interests would only be safe in an independent Sikh country of Khalistan. This was **further compounded** by an "incendiary mix of unprincipled politics and the manipulation of religious identities and institutions" that brought radical Sikh forces to the forefront of politics in the state of Punjab.

Violent clashes between radicalized Sikh groups led by Jarnail Singh Bhindranwale and the Nirankari sect (considered heretical by the former) in April 1978 is considered the beginning of the Khalistan movement. And in 1980, Bhindranwale and his supporters **started targeting Hindus** and murdered Lala Jagat Narain, the publisher of *Punjab Kesri*, a vernacular newspaper, and a vocal critic of Bhindranwale. This was soon followed by large scale violence against civilians across the state.

The Khalistan movement peaked in the 1980-90s and the violent campaign included bombings, assassinations, kidnappings, and selective killing and massacres of civilians. The movement resulted in nearly 22,000 deaths of Sikhs and Hindus alike, including approximately 12,000 civilians. The violence took on an international dimension in 1985 when Khalistani separatists based in Canada **exploded a bomb on an Air India flight** enroute from Toronto to New Delhi, killing all 329 people on board, including 82 children under the age of 13. That incident remains the deadliest terrorist attack in Canadian history.

According to **Human Rights Watch**, "Militants were responsible for numerous human rights abuses during the violent separatist struggle for an independent Khalistan, including the killings of Hindu and Sikh civilians, assassinations of political leaders, and the indiscriminate use of bombs leading to a large number of civilian deaths in Punjab and other parts of India. Under the cover of militancy, criminals began to coerce businessmen and landowners, demanding protection money."

As Canadian Political Science Professor, **Hamish Telford**, has also noted, "Over time, the Khalistan movement descended into thuggery. The militants increasingly engaged in robbery, extortion, rape, indiscriminate killings and ever-escalating terrorist attacks on innocent civilians. By 1991, Sikh militants were generally viewed as unprincipled criminal gangs."

In response to the movement, and in an attempt to end militancy in the state, Indian security forces and local Punjab police responded with force, at times committing human rights abuses. Moreover, the Congress Party led central government contributed to problems in the state by undermining democratic institutions and interfering with elections, and failing to adequately address local/state issues and relations between the state and the central government. It is important to note, however, that the majority of the police, security forces, and politicians in Punjab were and are Sikh. In fact, the police captain credited for ending the Khalistan insurgency, KPS Gill, was himself a Sikh. Moreover, Sikh politicians, such as former Chief Minister Beant Singh, were themselves **assassinated by militants**.

Violence Against Hindu and Sikh Civilians

The majority of the victims of the militant violence were innocent Sikhs who were killed by separatists for opposing the Khalistan movement. In 1990-1991, for instance, Sikh civilians comprised over seventy percent of the victims of militant attacks. Moreover, Mazhabi Sikhs (so called lower caste Sikhs in Punjab) were frequently the victims of militant attacks.

Hindus were also targeted in large numbers as part of a strategy to ignite communal tensions and force Hindus to flee Punjab in fear. Along with systematic violence, posters often appeared in villages threatening Hindus to leave and those Sikhs that sought to help Hindus were similarly threatened by militants. As a result, thousands of Hindus fled their homes in Punjab and lived as refugees in neighboring states and New Delhi.

Reports of grenades and bombs being thrown into Hindu religious festivals and movie theaters; militants firing indiscriminately into crowded markets; Hindus being pulled off busses and trains and massacred were common occurrences during that period. The following are a few representative examples of attacks on civilians that drew international attention:

May 1985 — Khalistani militants set off more than 30 bombs over the span of 14 hours at bus and train stations and public parks in New Delhi and the states of Punjab, Haryana, Rajasthan, and Uttar Pradesh, leaving at least 86 people dead.

December 1986 — 24 Hindu passengers were massacred and seven others wounded after being ordered off of a bus by militants near Khuda in Hoshiarpur district. In a similar incident, four months earlier, 15 Hindu passengers were slaughtered on a bus in Muktsar after militants told all the Sikh passengers to leave.

March 1988 — Militants killed 32 Hindus and injured 25 more when they opened fire on villagers celebrating the Hindu festival of Holi in Hoshiarpur district. 12 additional Hindus were killed in separate incidents the night before.

June 1989 — Two Sikh bus passengers were shot dead by militants for intervening and trying to save the lives of Hindu passengers.

November 1989 — 19 students were killed by militants while sleeping in a dormitory at Thapar Engineering College in the city of Patiala.

June 1991 — 125 men, women, and children were killed by Khalistan Commando Force militants on two trains. The first train was stopped near the city of Baddowal and militants opened fire indiscriminately on the train. A second train was stopped nearby where militants segregated Sikh and Hindu passengers, ordering Hindus off the train before killing them execution style.

May 1992 — All India Radio station director in Patiala, M.L. Manchanda was kidnapped and decapitated by Babbar Khalsa militants for failing to comply with an edict to only broadcast in Punjabi. The torso of Manchanda's **dead body** was left in Patiala, while his head was left in Ambala.

The Khalistan movement's campaign of violence further included attacks on those participating in **statewide elections in Punjab**. In February 1992, for instance, militants gunned down election workers, political campaigners, voters, and set off over 18 bombs.

Anti-Hindu Propaganda

The horrific violence in Punjab was accompanied by virulent anti-Hindu rhetoric and propaganda that demonized and intimidated the state's minority Hindu community, and encouraged and celebrated violence against Hindu civilians. This was part of an attempt by militants, led by Bhindranwale, to disrupt the social fabric of the state and creation divisions between Hindus and Sikhs, who had historically enjoyed strong relations, shared religious traditions, and frequently intermarried.

The **Dal Khalsa**, which gained notoriety for hijacking an Indian Airlines plane in 1981, placed severed cow heads at several Hindu temples in the state to intimidate Hindus, who consider cows to be sacred.

Bhindranwale, the most prominent Khalistan leader, frequently used anti-Hindu rhetoric in his speeches. Noted Sikh journalist, **Kushwant Singh**, described Bhindranwale as a "hate monger" who routinely used hateful and inflammatory language against Hindus and exhorted every Sikh to "kill 32 Hindus to solve the Hindu-Sikh problem."

Similarly, on July 28, 1984, Ajaib Singh Bagri, a leader in the Khalistani militant group, Babbar Khalsa International (BKI), **declared at a public rally in Canada** that "I give you my most solemn assurance that until we kill 50,000 Hindus, we will not rest!" The crowd of thousands of pro-Khalistan supporters responded with chants of "Hindu dogs! Death to them!"

BKI, along with International Sikh Youth Federation, were later designated as Specially Designated Global Terrorist (SDGT) organizations by the **US Department of State** under section 1(b) of Executive Order (E.O.) 13224.

Operation Bluestar

As the Khalistan movement expanded and violence escalated, Bhindranwale and his heavily armed followers **occupied the Golden Temple**, Sikhism's holiest shrine, in Amritsar. Starting in 1982, Bhindranwale used the Golden Temple as a base of operations and stored arms and ammunition there. He **openly declared** that he was directing attacks and violent acts from the sacred Temple. There were also reports of the militants committing atrocities on pilgrims and devotees inside the sacred space.

On June 6, 1984, Indian Prime Minister Indira Gandhi ordered an army operation — code-named Operation Bluestar — to flush out Bhindranwale and the militants holed up in the Golden Temple.

According to an **academic study** of the Khalistan insurgency:

"Bhindranwale established the center of his terror campaign in the Harimandir Sahib of Amritsar – the holiest of all Sikh temples. Many of his decisions and actions contravened the fundamental dogmas of the Sikh religion, but the faithful tolerated even this from him. He stockpiled arms and ammunition in the temple and from its sanctuary openly defied the state and federal governments. The police dared not enter the temple complex, because it did not want to provoke the Sikhs..."

"...thousands of pilgrims were in the Golden Temple grounds when the [army] assault began, and the insurgents used many of them as human shields. Bhindranwale and many of his associates were killed – but there were a very large number of civilian casualties as well. The insurgents made their goal crystal clear: to create an independent, sovereign Khalistan, where the Sikh religion informs governance, Sikh culture dominates and Punjabi is spoken."

The fallout from Operation Bluestar resulted in the assassination of Prime Minister Indira Gandhi and the subsequent anti-Sikh pogrom in New Delhi in October 1984 in response to Prime Minister Gandhi's assassination. The pogrom took the lives of over 3,000 innocent Sikhs.

While the Indian government and judiciary have taken some positive steps to prosecute and convict those leaders involved in planning and carrying out the violence, several individuals and high level government leaders have still not been brought to justice more than 30 years later. Collectively, Operation Blue Star, and the anti-Sikh pogrom of 1984 and lack of justice thereafter have left a deep psychological wound in the minds of many Sikhs, and have further fueled the Khalistan militant movement or support for it.

Subsequent to his death, Bhindranwale, along with other Khalistan militants, have been anointed by supporters as saints, saviors, and martyrs. To this day, **images of an armed Bhindranwale** almost always adorn pro-Khalistan websites, social media pages, and posters at events.

International Support for Khalistan

In both its heyday and today, the Khalistan movement has received financial and logistical support from pro-Khalistan separatists based in the United States, Canada, and the United Kingdom, as well as Pakistan's Inter-Services Intelligence (ISI) Agency.

In particular, according to Indian defence analyst, **Ajai Sahni**, Pakistan's ISI spy agency provided refuge, training, arms, and funding to Khalistani terrorist organizations and coordinated "their activities with Islamist terrorist organisations such as the Lashkar-e-Toiba and the Hizb-ul-Mujahideen, as well as with organised crime operators, and drug and weapons' smugglers who have assisted in the movement of men and materials across the border into Punjab."

Moreover, according to foreign affairs analyst **Christine Fair**, "[t]he involvement of the diaspora was an important dimension of the Sikh insurgency. Not only was it a source of diplomatic and financial support, it was also a factor in enabling Pakistan to get involved in fueling the Sikh separatist efforts. Sikhs in Canada, the United Kingdom, and the United States played important roles in arranging for cadres to travel to Pakistan, where they received financial and military assistance."

Khalistan supporters in the West have actively used American, Canadian, and British soil to lobby their respective governments against India, while **raising funds** for Khalistan terror groups, often using informal hawala networks (often used by criminal and terrorist organizations in South Asia) for transferring money.

There have further been a number of investigations into the activities of pro-Khalistan extremists in the US, including by the FBI, DEA, and United States Customs Service (USCS).

In March 2017, for instance, a Khalistan extremist and US resident, Balwinder Singh, was **convicted** of providing material support to Khalistani terrorist groups in India and sentenced to 15 years in federal prison. He had been arrested by the FBI in 2013 on "charges of conspiracy to provide material support to terrorists, conspiracy to murder or otherwise harm persons in a foreign country" and for falsifying an asylum claim. Singh was providing support to BKI and another group, Khalistan Zindabad Force, to commit acts of terrorism in India.

And previously, an undercover **USCS sting operation** of a Khalistan activist in California, Bhajan Singh Bhinder, revealed that he attempted to purchase military grade weapons, such as "M-16s, A.K.-47s, detonators, night-vision goggles, mobile communications equipment, remote-control equipment, grenade and rocket launchers," for Khalistan groups committing terror attacks in India. The investigation was later abandoned after Bhinder backed out of the deal. Bhinder has since gone on to found several other organizations, most notably **Organization for Minorities of India** (OFMI), which engages in anti-India and anti-Hindu activities.

Another US-based organization, **Sikhs for Justice**, has become the most prominent pro-Khalistan group in the west and reportedly enjoys the **support of the ISI**. It purportedly peacefully advocates for a 2020 referendum on Khalistan, but has **openly associated** with convicted Khalistan terrorists and those suspected of being involved in large-scale terror plots in India. It funded the **legal defense** of Jagtar Singh Tara, for instance, a leader of Indian designated terrorist group Khalistan Tiger Force, who assassinated the Chief Minister of India's Punjab state in 1995.

SFJ and its legal advisor, Gurpatwant Singh Pannun, also have close links with **Paramjit Singh Pamma**, a BKI fundraiser wanted by Indian authorities for his material support of terrorism. Mr. Pannun himself was reportedly arrested by police in the United Kingdom in 2000 after receiving terrorist training in Pakistan and was sentenced to 30 months in prison for his involvement with BKI, a banned terrorist group in the UK, although he denies the allegation.

12

Adam's Project (A Reality or A Myth?)

The historical Indian sculptures, monuments, and other landmarks are noteworthy and reflect the religious beliefs of the majority of the population. India, a country with a rich historical heritage, holds pride in its legacy and landmarks, such as the Taj Mahal and the Red Fort. The Ram Setu bridge is one such mythical monument. Ram Setu bridge is many centuries old and continues to be a hot topic among archaeologists, scientists, and people across the globe. Currently, a case is pending in the Supreme Court to brand the Ram Setu bridge as a national monument.

Ram Setu is one of the rare structures that serves as a bridge between mythology and history. In the Ramayana, the route Rama and his army took to get to Sri Lanka was through the **Rameshwaram bridge**, also known as **Adam's Bridge.** After putting in a lot of effort to bring back his wife Sita, Rama and his followers travelled from Rameswaram to Sri Lanka. With this belief, the Ram Setu bridge was built to cover the **India to Sri Lanka distance.**

Recently, the Indian government gave its approval for undersea research to analyse and establish the precise age of the India-Sri Lanka bridge. It will also concentrate on learning how this **Setu** came to be. In this study, the **Ram Setu bridge** was declared a national monument and has been concurrently ongoing and under dispute since 2005. Therefore, in light of everything above, it is now even more crucial to explore the potential connections between this Indian historic structure and the architecture of the modern period.

Facts About Ram Setu (Adam's Bridge)

- The causeway that covers the **India to Sri Lanka distance** is identical to the **Ram Setu,** also known as **Adam's Bridge.** The bridge runs from Mannar Island, in Sri Lanka, to Pamban Island, in Tamil Nadu, India.

- On a rough scale, this **Ram Setu bridge** is 50 kilometres long. Additionally, this bridge divides the Palk Strait from the Gulf of Mannar. The shallow seas surrounding the **Setu** range from 3 feet to 30 feet.

- Geology has also provided evidence that **Ram Setu** was a geographical connection between the two countries, India and Sri Lanka.

- Several scientific studies up until 1480 asserted that the **Adam's Bridge** was built above sea level. However, the bridge was damaged due to the devastation caused by the hurricane in that region. Until the cyclone hit that region, the bridge was accessible on foot.

- According to oceanography, the bridge is considered 7,000 years old or so. This information agrees with carbon dating on a beach near Dhanushkodi and Mannar Island.

- The Setusamudram Project was designed in 1860 by Alfred Dundas Taylor and recently approved by the Indian Government. This proposal was suggested as a quick route from Mannar Island to Pamban Island. However, as warned by environmentalists, this initiative has the potential to harm the natural reefs, which have existed for countless years. The

Setusamudram project was to be carried out using the Pamban Pass deepening. The **Ram Setu** won't sustain any harm in this manner. However, this project is currently pending.

Importance of Ram Setu in Mythology

The first reference to **Ram Setu** appears in the Hindu epic tale known as the Ramayana. This **Setu** is thought to have been built thanks to the efforts of Lord Rama's army, with guidance from Nala (a warrior monkey and the engineer behind the building of the **Setu**). The Rameshwaram bridge was built for Lord Rama to travel to Sri Lanka and save his wife Sita from King Ravana's imprisonment. According to Indian epic tradition, the **Rama Setu** was constructed using floating stones with the name of Lord Rama etched on them, rendering the stones unsinkable.

Other names for **Rama Setu** include Nala Setu, **Adam's Bridge**, and Setu Bandha.

The **Ram Setu** bridge is considered a notable historical and archaeological relic of the Ramayana. According to Hindu mythology, Ram Setu is a holy location. Therefore, building a bridge over this sacred location is not appropriate.

Is Ram Setu Man-Made?

Ram Setu bridge has been a topic of controversy for over four decades now. Many studies are currently being conducted to comprehend Ram Setu's genuine essence. However, recently there have been **Ram Setu images** from NASA, mostly satellite images that act as proof of evidence. According to the **Ram Setu images** from NASA, the stones across India and Sri Lanka are perched on a sandbar, commonly known as a shoal. While the investigators believe the sandbar is natural, the stones are not. **Ram Setu** may be a man-made bridge, as per the proof and belief of many. However, it is said that the **Rameshwaram bridge** was only visible until the 15th century.

Why is Ram Setu Known as Adam's Bridge?

Rameshwaram bridge was initially featured in Ibn Khordadbeh's Book of Roads and Kingdoms (c. 850). In this text,

Ram Setu is referred to as the "Bridge of the Sea." The **Setu** was given the name **"Adam's Bridge"** as Adam was using it to travel from Sri Lanka to India after being banished from Eden's Garden. In addition to this incident, a British cartographer named this region **Adam's Bridge** on a map he created in the year 1804.

The Expedition of Ram Setu Bridge

In March 2021, archaeologists and scientists performed the Setu mission. It was carried out to investigate the limestone chain of shoals that runs between Rameshwaram in India and Sri Lanka. This project aims to comprehend the characteristics of the limestone rocks as well as the geological evolution of the rocks and other distinctive features of the 8-kilometre-long **Ram Setu.** Over the past few years, the Indian Council of Historical Research has received countless proposals. But this is the first proposal that the board has approved.

In addition, the board has allocated enough funds for the bridge's expedition. The primary goal of the mission is to determine whether the **Setu** is artificial and to end the protracted discussion around this mythical bridge.

ASI Approves Further Research on Ram Setu Bridge

The proposal for **Ram Setu's** investigation has been authorised by the Central Advisory Board of Archaeology, a government organisation established under the Archaeology Survey of India (ASI) in 2021. The **Rama Setu bridge's** creation date and method are being uncovered through this investigation. The underwater research began in 2021.

The Council for Scientific and Industrial Research (CSIR) is in charge of researching the **Ram Setu bridge.** Along with CSIR, the National Institute of Oceanography (NIO), a Goa-based organisation, is concentrating on this research to learn every aspect of the creation of the **Adam's Bridge**, including how it was built. The study will also examine a few additional issues, such as any possible submerged settlements near the bridge.

The National Institute of Oceanography's research ship, designated "Sindhu Sankalp" or "Sindhu Sadhana," is being used to explore this project by collecting sediment samples from at least 35 to 40 metres below sea level. This study is primarily grounded in archaeological findings and geologically dated artefacts.

Additionally, radiometric techniques are being utilised to establish the precise age of the **Ram Setu bridge**, which is thought to be made of coral and pumice stones. Calcium carbonate is one of the minerals found in these corals. The age of the **Ram Setu bridge** can be precisely determined with the use of these minerals.

Ram Setu Bridge: Mysterious Facts About the Structure

Even after the controversy over whether or not the **Ram Setu** is man-made, no substantial piece of proof has been located. There are a few mysterious truths regarding the bridge that you might not be aware of. Here are a few of them:

· Nala Setu, or **Adam's Bridge**, is another name for **Rama Setu**. The former name of this **Setu** was drawn from Islamic scripture, where it first appeared. The existence of Adam's Peak in Sri Lanka has been mentioned in this Islamic literature. Since the architect who created the limestone shoal bridge was named Nala (a warrior monkey from the Ramayana), this bridge is also known as Nala Setu.

· The carbon dating of beaches and studies of oceanography has indicated a period that corresponds with the Ramayana's chronological period and is said to be 7,000 years old.

· In the Ramayana, it is mentioned that floating stones were used to build the **Ram Setu bridge**. Strangely, these floating stones are still visible throughout Rameswaram today. According to scientific theories, most volcanic stones float in water. This may help to explain why the rocks that make up this bridge are arranged in a line.

· The **Adam's Bridge** is submerged underwater, yet ships cannot navigate across it. The depth of the water here varies at several locations, making it shallow. Thus, ships from India must travel a different detour to reach Sri Lanka.

Sethusamudram Project and the Supreme Court

A petition was signed and sent to the Supreme Court asking for **Ram Setu's** protection by Dr. Swammy in 2007. To pursue the petition, the Supreme Court asked the Indian government if it wanted to take the **Rama Setu** out of the Setusamudram project. The government assured the court that the **Ram Setu** would not be harmed or touched by this project. In addition to the plea, Dr. Swamy addressed the topic of classifying **Ram Setu** as a National Heritage Monument, but the Top Court issued a stay order on the project's work over **Ram Sethu.**

The Sethusamudram project called for massive excavation and removal of the limestone shoals that make up the mythical **Setu** to create an 83-km long deep-water channel connecting Mannar with Palk Strait. The two nations will build a shipping canal to establish the connection. The sea that separates India and Sri Lanka is known as Setusamudram, and its depth is less than 10 metres. India still lacks a continuous canal for navigation connecting the country's east and west coasts because the area is too shallow. The SSCP suggested building a waterway directly linking India's two coasts. Additionally, this will shorten the travel time between Chennai and Cape Comorin.

Furthermore, it will aid in stopping the ships from being turned around and sailing directly toward Sri Lanka. As a result, the Setusamudram Shipping Canal Project will also help to shorten the typical travel time between the coasts.

In 2022, on July 26, Dr. Subramanian Swamy, a Rajya Sabha member, asked for an expedited hearing on his request from the Centre to declare **Ram Setu** a national historical monument, and the verdict is still pending.

13

Netaji Death

Netaji Subash Chandra Bose's death is still shrouded in mystery. But the various conspiracy theories about it make it even more mysterious. While recently the news about Gumnami Baba, a revered saint of Faizabad, Uttar Pradesh, who was believed to be Bose himself, came to the fore, we never cease to imagine how the great man must have spent his last moments on earth.

Here is a look back at some of the most intriguing conspiracy theories:

At 2 PM on August 17, 1945, a Mitsubishi Ki-21 heavy bomber took off from Saigon airport. Inside the aircraft were 13 people, including Lt Gen Tsunamasa Shidei of the Imperial Japanese Army, Col Habibur Rahman of the Indian National Army and one man who sat in a seat a little behind the portside wing – Netaji Subhas Chandra Bose.

After an overnight halt in Vietnam, on August 18, the plane arrived to refuel in Taihoku, Formosa (now Taipei, Taiwan). Moments after the flight took off again, passengers heard a loud 'bang'. Ground crew saw the portside engine fall off, and the plane crashed. The pilots and Lt Gen Shidei were killed instantly, Col Rahman fell unconscious. Bose survived, but his gasoline-soaked clothes ignited, turning him into a human torch.

The Mitsubishi Ki-21 twin-engine heavy bomber that Netaji Subhas Chandra Bose and Col Habibur Rahman boarded at Saigon airport around 2 PM on 17 August 1945. Image courtesy: Wikimedia A few hours later, in coma in a hospital, Netaji Subhas Chandra Bose passed away.

This is the established account of how one of India's most famous freedom fighters died.

But is it true?

"There were no official reports released by the Governments of India or Britain," historian Leonard Gordon says, "Even members of India's Interim Government in 1946 waffled on the matter. Bose had disappeared several times earlier in his life; so rumours began again in 1945 and a powerful myth grew."

What you will read next is a saga of secrets, political vendetta, outrageous claims, half-truths and full rumours that strive to prove that Netaji did not die on that fateful day in Taiwan.

No dead body

In the immediate aftermath, an intriguing, and perhaps damning fact emerged: Netaji's other lieutenants, who were to follow him on another flight, never saw his body. No one took photographs of Bose's injuries, or his body, nor was a death certificate issued.

Netaji with Mahatma Gandhi. Image courtesy: wallpics.biz

As news reached India, senior INA officer JR Bhonsle rejected the news. Mahatma Gandhi said, "Subhas is not dead. He is still alive and biding his time somewhere."

Soon, rumours began doing the rounds that Bose was either in Soviet-held Manchuria, a prisoner of the Soviet Army, or had gone into hiding in Russia. Lakshmi Swaminathan, of the INA's Jhansi Regiment, said in 1946 she thought Bose was in China.

The Sadhu story

In the 1950s, there emerged stories that Netaji had become a sadhu. And, the most elaborate of these took shape a decade later. Some of Netaji's old associates formed the 'Subhasbadi Janata', and claimed Bose was now the chief sadhu in an ashram in Shoulmari in North Bengal.

Through well-crafted newspapers and magazines, the organisation was able to, quite convincingly, recreate Bose's post-war activities.

According to the 'Subhasbadis', Bose returned to India after the war, became a sadhu, attended Gandhi's funeral unseen in 1948, lived in a temple in Bareilly in the late 1950s, before finally settling in Shoulmari as Srimat Saradanandaji in 1959.

Other versions, too, began gathering credence. Bose remained either in Maoist China or the Soviet Union. He attended Jawaharlal Nehru's cremation in 1964, of which there appeared to even be photographic evidence.

Neta jee with Jawahar Lal Nehru
May 27 1964

Image courtesy: nigamrajendra28 blogspot.in

There were claims that Soviet leader Nikita Khrushchev told an interpreter in Delhi that the Soviet Union could produce Bose in 45 days if India so desired.

The Soviet Connection and a Conspiracy

After independence, Nehru took the Foreign Affairs portfolio himself and appointed Vijayalekshmi Pandit as the ambassador to Russia. After her term ended, Dr S. Radhakrishnan took her place.

There are reports that Dr Saroj Das, of Calcutta University, told his friend Dr RC Muzumdar that Dr Radhakrishnan had told him that Bose was in Russia.

Radhakrishnan met Netaji in Moscow, says witness

Calcutta, Nov. 16 (UNI)—Mr S. M. Goswami, a retired special officer of the anti-Corruption Department of the West Bengal Government, told the Netaji Inquiry Commission here today that Dr S. Radhakrishnan, the former President of India, had told him in 1954 in New Delhi that Netaji Subhas Chandra Bose met him (Dr Radhakrishnan) in Moscow in 1948 when he had gone there as a member of a delegation to a philosophical conference.

Mr Goswami said Dr Radhakrishnan had told him that Netaji Bose had asked him (Dr Radhakrishnan) to make arrangements for his (Bose's) return to India. Mr Goswami quoted Dr Radhakrishnan as saying, "I told the bighups about this but they did not like this to be disclosed."

Mr Goswami said Dr Radhakrishnan had told him all these when he (Goswami) presented a copy of his book titled "Netaji Mystery" to him (Dr Radhakrishnan).

When Dr Radhakrishnan came to Calcutta as the President of India on July 1, on the death of Dr B. C. Roy, Dr Radhakrishnan had "reaffirmed" this, Mr Goswami said.

He said when he requested Dr Radhakrishnan to make a "public statement" in this regard the then President said, "Goswami, if I make a statement and Netaji does not come what will be my position you realise."

Mr Goswami said he then pledged to Dr Radhakrishnan that so long as he remained the President of India, he (Goswami) would not disclose what he had told him.

"If Dr Radhakrishnan denies it now, I will commit suicide before him," he declared.

Replying to a question from the commission chairman, Mr Justice G. D. Khosla, Mr Goswami said Mrs Vijayalakshmi Pandit, former Indian Ambassador to Russia, had also seen Netaji in Moscow.

Witness said that on her return to India, Mrs Pandit said at the Constitution House that she had some "important" information which, "if I disclose, will electrify the whole of India."

At this stage, Mr Nehru "made her sit by pulling her sari," he said.

Show-cause notice on IAS officer

Hindustan Times Correspondent
Lucknow, Nov. 16—The Gov-

Hindustan Times news report, Nov 17, 1970. Image courtesy: bp.blogspot.com

In another report, former Indian ambassador Dr Satyanarayana Sinha met CPI founder Abani Mukherjee's son Georgey, who said his father and Netaji were imprisoned in adjacent cells in Siberia.

In 1995, a team from Calcutta's Asiatic Society, researching Indo-Soviet ties in Moscow, found a bunch of declassified files that hinted at Bose having been in the USSR after 1945. Dr Purobi Roy, a member of the team of scholars, said she found a document stamped "most secret", dated 1946, in the military archives of Paddolosk, near Moscow, which mentioned Stalin and Molotov discussing Bose's plans — whether he would remain in the USSR or leave.

Dr Roy also said she found a KGB report in Bombay from 1946, which said, "it is not possible to work with Nehru or Gandhi, we have to use Subhas Bose". This implies Bose was still alive in 1946.

This photograph allegedly shows water room-heaters behind Netaji. These heaters were in use only in the USSR at the time. Image courtesy: thesundayindian.com

Gumnami Baba, aka 'Bhagwanji'

Of all this, the most enduring legend is of a sadhu in Faizabad whom the locals called Gumnami Baba, who went by the name Bhagwanji. Bhagwanji, they say, was a monk who lived in Uttar Pradesh – Lucknow, Faizabad, Sitapur, Basti and Ayodhya – for more than 30 years till his death on September 16, 1985. He maintained contact with Dr Pavitra Mohan Roy, the former top Secret Service agent of the INA.

However, more than his life, what Bhagwanji left behind after his death seems to confirm that the sadhu and Bose were one and the same: Gold-rimmed spectacles identical to what Netaji was always pictured wearing, powerful German binoculars, a colour photograph of Swami Vivekananda, Bengali books, the original copy of the summons issued to Suresh Chandra Bose to appear before the Khosla Commission, a map of undivided India, an album containing family photographs of Netaji Subhas Chandra Bose.

Left: Netaji's handwriting. Right: Bhagwanji's handwriting. Forensic expert Dr B Lal told the Mukherjee Commission that both handwritings matched. Image courtesy: nigamrajendra28.blogspot.in

Other items recovered included a torch pencil generally used in map-making by military personnel, newspaper clippings about Netaji's 'death' probe, letters from Netaji's followers.

One of the more intriguing finds was a letter from a person who accompanied the Khosla Commission to Taiwan, which reads: "We got only 15 days in Taihoku (Taipei). Formosa's (Taiwan) task is over... I cannot write everything in this letter, if you permit, I can come over for a week."

Photographs found among Bhagwanji's belongings indicate he celebrated his birthday on January 23.

There was no plane crash

Clipping from a Japanese newspaper, published on August 23, 1945, reporting the death of Bose and General Tsunamasa Shidei. Image courtesy: Wikimedia

Netaji could not have died in a plane crash because no aviation accident occurred in Taipei on August 18, 1945.

In 2005, the BBC reported that not only did the Taiwanese government reject the Bose-died-in-a-plane-crash-in-Taipei story, it also denied any plane crashes occurred between August 14 and September 20 that year.

Stalin killed Netaji

Most recently, the BJP's Subramanian Swamy has alleged that Bose did not actually die in a plane crash in 1945, but was killed by Soviet dictator Josef Stalin in 1953.

"According to the papers that exist with us, Bose had faked his death and escaped to Manchuria in China which was under Russian occupation, hoping Russia would look after him. But Stalin put him in a jail in Siberia. Somewhere around 1953, he hanged or suffocated Bose to death," said Swamy, demanding that the Netaji files be declassified.

However, he conceded, "Declassification of Netaji documents in haste and without judging the consequences would be difficult. India's relations with Britain and Russia may be affected.

"But I will persuade the Prime Minister to disclose the documents."

Inquiries and Commissions

The Figgess Report of 1946, the first official probe into Bose's death, said: "As a result of a series of interrogations of individuals named in the following paragraphs it is confirmed as certain that S.C. Bose died in a Taihoku Military Hospital (Nammon Ward) sometime between 1700 hours and 2000 hours local time on the August 18, 1945. The cause of death was heart failure resulting from multiple burns and shock."

In sum, the Figgess Report confirms:

1. The crash near Taihoku airport on August 18, 1945, in which Subhas Chandra Bose was a passenger

2. Bose's death in a nearby military hospital on the same day

3. Bose's cremation in Taihoku

4. Transfer of Bose's ashes to Tokyo

The Shah Nawaz Committee of 1956 was India's first inquiry, comprising three people – Member of Parliament Shah Nawaz Khan, West Bengal government-nominated ICS officer SN Maitra, and Suresh Chandra Bose, Bose's elder brother.

The committee interviewed 67 witnesses in India, Japan, Thailand and Vietnam, including the 'survivors' of the plane crash. Most importantly, it interviewed Colonel Habibur Rahman, Bose's companion on the flight. Based on these testimonies, Khan and Maitra concluded Bose had died in a plane crash in Taipei.

The committee's third member, Netaji's brother, however, disputed the report, claiming Jawaharlal Nehru orchestrated the inquiry to infer death by plane crash.

'Gandhi, others had agreed to hand over Netaji'

Bombay, Jan. 22 (PTI)—Mr Usman Patel, who claimed to be a bodyguard of Netaji Subhash Chandra Bose, said here today that Mahatma Gandhi, Mr Jawaharlal Nehru, Mr Mohamed Ali Jinnah and Maulana Azad had come to an agreement with the British judge that if Netaji were to enter India, he would be handed over and charged.

Mr Patel told Mr G. D. Khosla, the one-man Inquiry Commission on the concluding day of the three-day sitting here, that Maulana Azad had later confirmed this. Mr Patel said Mr Azad had told him that he was going to write a book and that he would mention this matter in it.

Later, Mr Patel continued, the voluntarily gave a report of this to Dharmayug, a Bombay weekly, because he read that the Commission was inquiring into Netaji's disappearance.

False report

Mr Patel who broke tears while giving evidence said Mr Nehru had asked him to make an application falsely stating that the $21,600 (Singapore) seized from him when he was arrested on Oct. 15, 1945, was his own and that he was trading in rubber in Singapore. The money belonged to Netaji for purchasing ration and foodstuff for the Indian National Army, he said.

Mr Patel said he did not relate the story of Netaji's disappearance and the burning of the aircraft and its crash to anybody including

Mahatma Gandhi and Mr Nehru because the country was not dependent then. He had disclosed these to Mr Nehru when he heard that the Shah Nawaz Khan Committee was going to Tokyo to investigate the disappearance of Netaji. This he did because Mr Shah Nawaz Khan did not permit him to appear before the Committee.

Mr Patel said Mr Nehru had told him that he would arrange to send him (Mr Patel) with the Committee. Mr Govindrao Deshpande, MP, from Nasik was present when the conversation took place, Mr Patel said.

Dr Suresh Pathye, Capt R. B. Wirmani and Dr M. A. Jamal disposed at the hearing about their association with Netaji.

The Commission will meet in New Delhi on a four-day hearing from March 1 and it may go over to Tokyo by the middle of March, according to Mr Khosla.

Col. Habib-ur-Rehman, one of the important witnesses, would be examined either in New Delhi or in Pakistan where he resides, the court said.

Order on Bengal I-G contested

Calcutta, Jan. 22 (UND)—The Union of India today filed an appeal in the Calcutta High Court against the order of Mr Justice Sabyasachi Mukherjee setting aside the orders of appointment of the West Bengal Inspector-General of Police, Mr P. K. Basu.

Hindustan Times news report, Jan 21, 1971. Image courtesy: quora.com

14 years later, the Government of India sanctioned another inquiry, this time by a one-man team – the Khosla Commission of 1970. Deposing before the Khosla Commission, Dr Satyanarayan Sinha had said Colonel Habibur Rehman had confessed to him in 1946 that he lied about Bose dying in a plane crash.

However, the commission chose to concur with the two preceding inquiries into Bose's death.

More than 25 years later, yet another Government of India enquiry was constituted — this time, however, by a BJP-led government. In 1999, the Mukherjee Commission, led by retired Supreme Court judge MK Mukherjee, began his exhaustive probe into the Bose mystery.

In 2005, after perusing hundreds of documents, taking oral testimonies, and visits to Japan, Russia and Taiwan, the commission reported that the Japanese and the USSR made a secret plan to grant Bose safe passage into the USSR. The commission also said that the ashes kept at Renkoji Temple, believed to be Bose's, actually were of a Japanese soldier who died of a heart attack.

'Japanese had altered Netaji's flight plan'

New Delhi, Oct. 19 (UNI)—Mr Deb Nath Dass, formerly general secretary of the Indian Independence League in South-East Asia, told the Khosla Commission today that Netaji Subhash Chandra Bose had mentioned to him on the night of August 16, 17, 1945, that the Japanese had changed their plan regarding his departure from Saigon at the eleventh hour.

Appearing as a witness beforet the Commission inquiring into the disappearance of Netaji Bose, Mr Dass quoted Netaji Bose as telling him and some Indian National Army officers, who were present at the time, that the Japanese wanted to take him to Tokyo instead of to Manchuria.

He and some imporant INA officers present at Saigon did not like the idea and asked high Japanese officers where Netaji Bose was being taken. The Japanese replied: "Don't worry. You will also be taken to the same place where he is going." They, however, refused to reveal the name of the place, Mr Dass added.

Mr Dass was the last witness to give evidence before Mr Justice G. D. Khosla on the Commission's sittings in Delhi.

Mr Dass replied in the negative to a question by Mr Khosla whether Netaji had expressed his dislike to the idea of going to a place where the Japanese wanted to take him but said, "it appeared to me as though Netji was not happy at the change of destination."

Mr Dass said Netaji had carried 18 metal boxes containing treasures belonging to the Provisional Government of Azad Hind, which he had brought on August 16, 1945, to Bangkok from Rangoon in a leather suit case. They included ornaments and cash donated to Netaji by Indians at various places in Southeast Asia. They were earlier kept in the National Azad Hind Bank.

The UPA government rejected the report in Parliament without citing any reason.

14
First AirCraft In India

The claim goes that, in 1895, a person called **Shivkar Bapuji Talpade** made a heavier-than-air powered flight over Chowpatty beach - 9 years before the Wright Brothers. He supposedly built the plane under guidance of Subbaraya Shastry and his work, the **Vaimanika Shastra**. The unmanned plane was called *Marutsakha* (friend of Maruti).

The details of this flight are unclear. It is alleged that the craft was airborne for 18 minutes, and went as high as 200 meters or according to K.N.R.Swamy, 500 meters. For a feat so spectacular, the newspaper coverage or other contemporary accounts are almost none. Kesari, a marathi daily carried a report, but it was small and without any image or design. The Maharaja of Baroda, Sayajirao Gaekwad and Justice Ranade are said to witness the feat, but the mention doesn't go further than that.

Photography was quite developed by the time, and especially since the Maharaja was present, they should've taken a photo or something. Not just the incident, but there is no photograph, drawing or design details of the craft even after it. It reportedly was kept at his home even after his death.

If it had really flown, it would have been a big deal indeed, especially in a place like Mumbai it would not be an obscure news. The British technicians would promptly have taken advantage of it, and use it to their benefit. Looks like Talpade came to fame after mentions in another books in 20th century (see wiki).

The Vaimanika Shastra

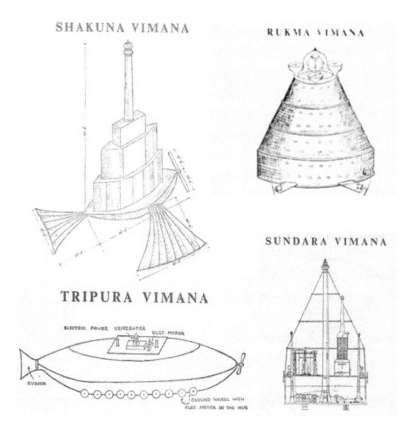

Enter Caption

It supposedly was built according to the Vaimanika Shastra, a 7000 year (claimed) treatise by Sage Bharadwaja, and transmitted by psychic channeling to Pandit Shastry. Studies say that the treatise is a recent 20th century work, and has no vedic origin.

Jayant Narlikar, a renowned astrophysicist who also happens to be a Sanskrit scholar, states that the author "lacks complete understanding of basic aerodynamics" and they would not fly. (in his book *Hyala Jeevan Aise Naav*)

It was critically examined by researchers from IISc, and they found the planes described in it unfeasible. Read the whole report here: Page on iisc.ernet.in

To quote from it,

The science of aeronautics requires an understanding of a number of disciplines: aerodynamics, aeronautical structures, propulsive devices, materials, and metallurgy. The subject works lay uncalled for emphasis on propulsive devices and structures, but little or no emphasis on aerodynamics. It is worth pointing out that the history of aeronautics (western) in regard to production of heavier-than-air craft is studded with initial failures, significantly traceable to a non-understanding of aerodynamics.

There is no discussion about aerodynamics, the author merely goes on about propulsion and the materials. The dimensions given to some planes are insane - as big as 1000 feet, and so are the speeds - 8000 mph, 625 mph. The materials used are metals like "Raja Loha", elephant's urine mixed with mercury, cow's urine, donkey's urine, etc.

The mercury propellant is first vapourised fed into the thruster discharge chamber ionised converted into plasma by a combination with electrons broke down electrically and then gyro armature accelerated through small openings in a screen to pass out of the engine at velocities between extremely great speeds. Ionization of air shifts every colour of the spectrum and invisibilty can be achieved.

Violation of Newton's Law:

The author states the plane will go in the *same direction* as the "jet goes out of the shundala" which is complete opposite of what happens.

The fast movement of the plane takes place in the same direction in which the jet gets out of shundala..

No details about mass:
There is *nothing* written about the masses of the planes or even their components, which is plain ridiculous.

Unintelligible units:
The text uses 'vitasti' for length, 'link' for speed, 'kaksha' for heat, & 'link' again for electrical force. The units of speed and temperature are new and, do not have any easily decipherable meaning. They did not even need the unit of mass.

Conclusion:
It is possible that Shree Talpade was a enthusiatic mechanic who tried to do something, but likely it failed. The Vaimanika Shastra looks more like fantasy than a working manual.

Thank You

Thank You for reading...
Do Follow me on Instagram
@restlessbrute